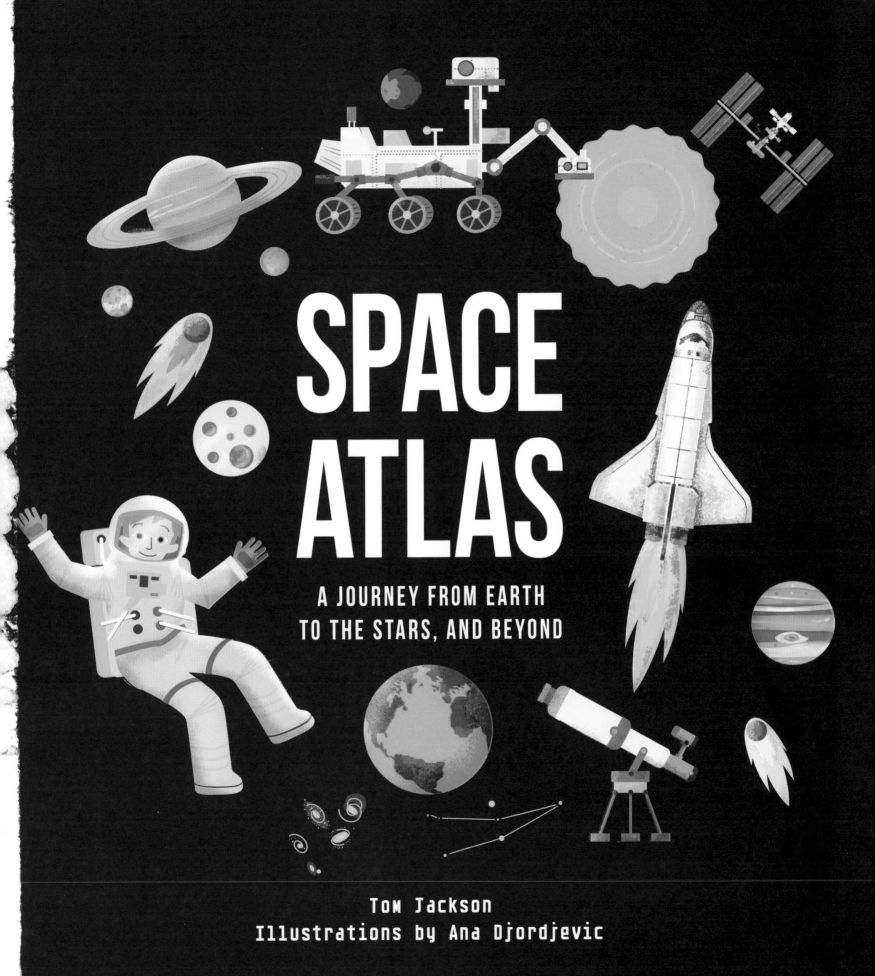

SPACE ATLAS

A JOURNEY FROM EARTH TO THE STARS, AND BEYOND

Tom Jackson

Illustrations by Ana Djordjevic

QEB

Quarto is the authority on a wide range of topics.

Quarto educates, entertains and enriches the lives of our readers—enthusiasts and lovers of hands-on livin

www.quartoknows.com

Author: Tom Jackson
Illustrator: Ana Djordjevic
Consultant: David Hawksett
Editor: Claudia Martin
Designer: Tracy Killick
QEB Editor: Ellie Brough
QEB Designer: Victoria Kimonidou

© 2018 Quarto Publishing plc

First published in 2018 by QEB Publishing,
an imprint of The Quarto Group.
6 Orchard Road, Suite 100,
Lake Forest, CA 92630.
T: +1 949 380 7510
F: +1 949 380 7575
www.QuartoKnows.com

A CIP record for this book is available from the Library of Congress.

ISBN: 978-1-912413-76-8

Manufactured in Shenzhen, China HH052018

9 8 7 6 5 4 3 2 1

PICTURE CREDITS

Shutterstock/Amanda Carden 4cl; NASA/JPL-Caltech/Harvard-Smithsonian CfA 7tr; Ocean Biology Processing Group at NASA's Goddard Space Flight Center 8br; Shutterstock/Tristan3D/Aphelleon 13tr; NASA/Johns Hopkins University Applied Physics Laboratory/Arizona State University/Carnegie Institution of Washington 16br; Getty Images/Sovfoto/UIG 18cr; NASA, modifications by Seddon 20tr; Kudinov Konstantin 22cr; NASA/JPL-Caltech/SwRI/MSSS/Betsy Asher Hall/Gervasio Robles 24tr; NASA/JPL/Space Science Institute 27tl; Erich Karkoschka (University of Arizona) and NASA/ESA 28tr; NASA/JPL 30tr; NASA/Johns Hopkins University Applied Physics Laboratory/Southwest Research Institute 33tr; Joshua Tree National Park/Brad Sutton 35tr; ESA/Rosetta/NAVCAM 35br; Y. Beletsky (LCO)/ESO 36tr; NASA/ESA/C.R. O'Dell (Vanderbilt University) 40br; Rogelio Bernal Andreo 42br; Smithsonian Institution 44tr; Harel Boren 48bl; NASA 48br; NASA 49tr; Shutterstock/Denis Belitsky 50bl; NASA/CXC/MIT/F. Baganoff, R. Shcherbakov et al. 52br; NASA/JPL-Caltech 55bl; ESA/Hubble & NASA 56br; NASA/Chris Gunn 59bc; NASA/WMAP Science Team 60tr

Words in **bold** are explained in the glossary on page 62.

CONTENTS

Journey with me to planets, stars, and distant galaxies. We will be the first humans ever to travel further than our Moon! 3-2-1... Blast off!

INTRODUCTION

Let's set off on a journey through space. We will leave Earth far behind as we travel to **planets**, **stars**, swirling **galaxies**, **black holes**, and into the depths of the Universe.

You can take a look at some places we will visit. Wait for a clear, dark night, then go outside and look up. Once the bright **Sun** goes down, you can see out into deep space. Most of those tiny dots are stars, burning brightly like our Sun, but **trillions** of miles away. The light from these stars has been traveling toward Earth for years and years, and only now has it reached your eyes for you to see.

SPACE SCIENCE

Scientists who study the Universe are called astronomers. No astronomer has traveled to another star or planet. Everything they know about the Universe comes from looking at the light and other waves of energy it gives out. In ancient times, astronomers watched the way stars moved night after night. They saw that some lights moved along different paths from the rest. These wandering lights are the planets, such as Mars.

In the 2nd century, Greek astronomer Ptolemy studied the planets and stars.

CONSTELLATIONS

Our ancestors gave names to the patterns they saw in the stars. The ancient Greeks named many of these **constellations** after characters from their myths. They included heroes like Hercules and creatures such as Draco the dragon and Ursa Major, the "Great Bear." Modern astronomers use many of the same patterns as the Greeks, dividing the sky into 88 constellations.

Aquarius

Capricorn

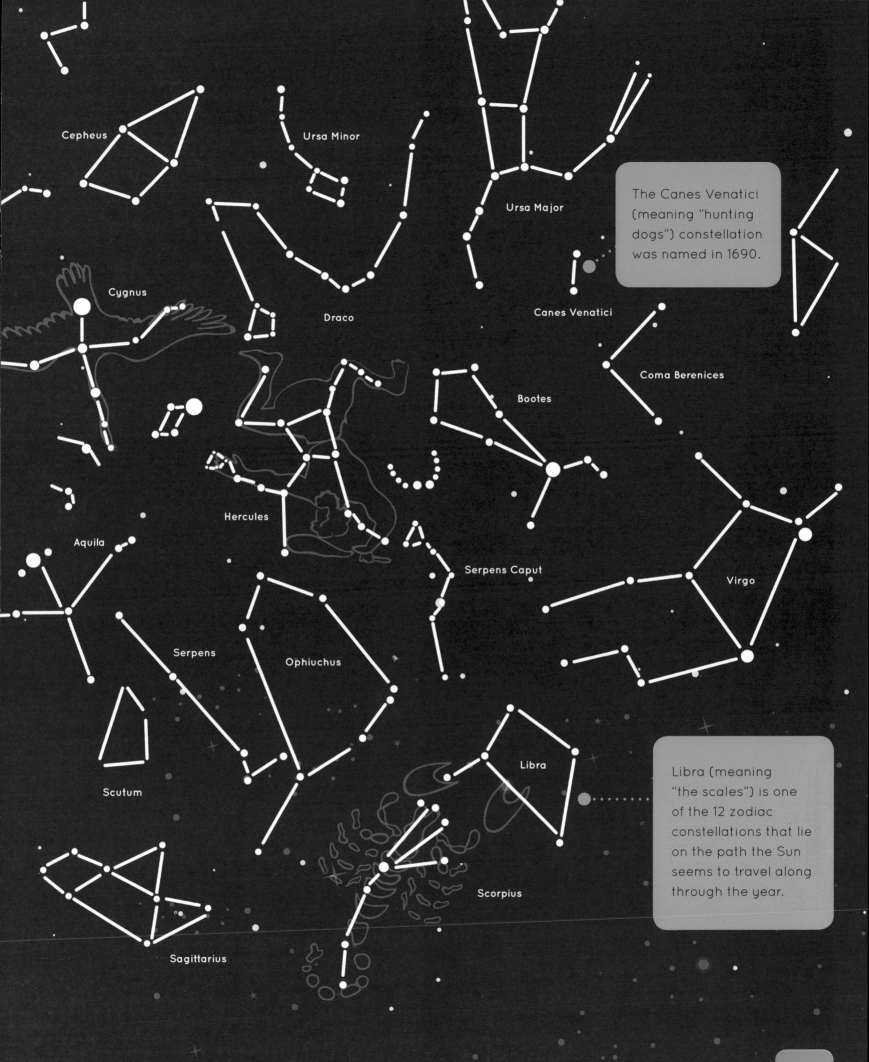

Cepheus

Ursa Minor

Ursa Major

The Canes Venatici (meaning "hunting dogs") constellation was named in 1690.

Cygnus

Draco

Canes Venatici

Coma Berenices

Bootes

Hercules

Serpens Caput

Virgo

Aquila

Serpens

Ophiuchus

Libra

Libra (meaning "the scales") is one of the 12 zodiac constellations that lie on the path the Sun seems to travel along through the year.

Scutum

Scorpius

Sagittarius

SIZING UP THE UNIVERSE

The Universe is as big as it gets. It contains everything that exists, as far as we know. To understand how vast the Universe is, and where all the stars and planets are located, astronomers have come up with ways of measuring the huge distances through space. First of all, let's get to grips with where Earth is in this amazing Universe:

Earth is in our **Solar System**. This is where Earth, the other planets, the **asteroids**, and comets are whizzing around the Sun.

The Sun is one of hundreds of **billions** of stars in a great swirling mass called the **Milky Way**, which is our galaxy.

Galaxies are not spread evenly through space—they cluster together. Our galaxy is in a cluster called the Local Group.

Galaxy clusters also cluster together, making superclusters. Our supercluster is called the Virgo Supercluster.

The Virgo Supercluster is just one of 10 million superclusters in the Universe!

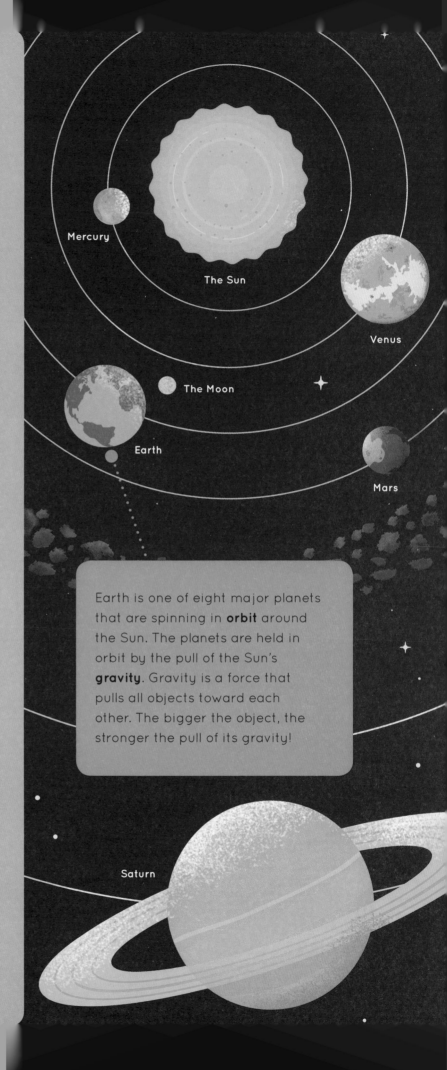

Mercury

The Sun

Venus

The Moon

Earth

Mars

Saturn

Earth is one of eight major planets that are spinning in **orbit** around the Sun. The planets are held in orbit by the pull of the Sun's **gravity**. Gravity is a force that pulls all objects toward each other. The bigger the object, the stronger the pull of its gravity!

STAR COUNT

No one knows the exact number of stars, but an estimate is 70 trillion billion. That's a 7 with 22 zeroes! Our Sun is one of those stars. On a clear night, away from bright city lights, you can see perhaps 2,000 stars. Powerful **telescopes** have spotted millions more, but that still leaves billions of stars that are too far away to see, even though many are blazing brighter than our Sun.

The *Spitzer Space Telescope* took this photo of stars that are around 400 light-years from Earth.

The Solar System is around 174 billion miles across.

Jupiter

Uranus

Neptune

SPACE MEASURES

When astronomers use feet and miles to measure distances in space, the numbers get very large. For example, the distance to the Sun from Earth is 490,828,800,000 feet. Instead, distances inside the Solar System are measured in **astronomical units** (AUs). Earth is exactly 1 AU from the Sun.

The distance from the Earth to the Sun is 1 astronomical unit (AU).

Outside the Solar System, distances are measured in **light-years**. One light-year is the distance light travels in a year: 31,168,000,000,000,000 feet.

The distance traveled by light in one year is 1 light-year.

EARTH

Earth is a very special planet because it is the only place in the Universe known to be home to living things, such as pineapples, poodles, and people. All living things need water to survive, and Earth has plenty of that...

The way we measure time comes from the movement of Earth. Our day and night are caused by our planet turning once every 24 hours. Any spot on Earth's surface is lit up by the Sun for roughly half that time. As the planet spins around, the Sun disappears from view. Our year is the time it takes for Earth to move around the Sun once—roughly 365 days.

SIZE: 7,926 miles across

WEIGHT: 6.6 trillion billion tons

DAY: 24 hours

YEAR: 365 days

DISTANCE FROM THE SUN: 1 AU

ATMOSPHERE: Nitrogen, oxygen, argon

MOONS: 1

ORBIT

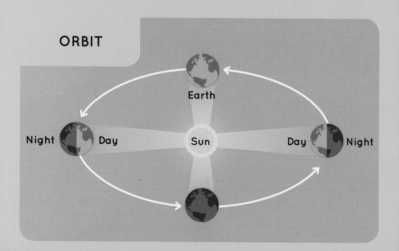

Night · Day · Earth · Sun · Day · Night

Around 70 percent of Earth's surface is covered in water. Life on Earth began in the oceans.

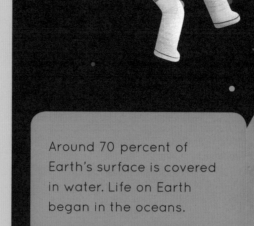

EARTH'S ATMOSPHERE

The scientific word for the air that surrounds Earth is the **atmosphere**. Most of Earth's air is in a layer about 6 miles high. Water is mixed into this air as water vapor, an invisible gas. Tiny droplets of water form clouds. Above this layer, the atmosphere gets thinner and thinner as it reaches out into space.

This photograph of Earth, taken by a satellite, shows clouds of water droplets swirling in the atmosphere.

The mantle is a region of hot, mushy rock called magma.

The outer **core** is liquid metal.

The Earth's inner core is a hot ball of solid metal, mostly iron and nickel.

GOLDILOCKS ORBIT

Earth is the only place in the Solar System where water is sloshing on the surface. Astronomers call Earth's position in the Solar System the "Goldilocks Orbit" because it is "not too hot and not too cold, but just right," like Baby Bear's porridge in "Goldilocks and the Three Bears." Water is only a liquid when the temperature is between 32 °F and 212 °F. Earth is the right distance from the Sun to be warm enough for water not to freeze, but not so hot that the oceans boil into steam.

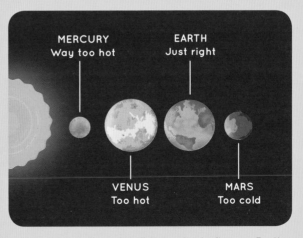

Earth's orbit is "just right" for water to flow on Earth, as rivers, lakes, seas, and falling rain.

THE ISS

The International Space Station, or ISS, is our permanent home in space. There is always someone on board, every day of the year, orbiting Earth 250 miles above.

The ISS is run by 16 countries, and its crew members come from all over the world. It took 13 years to complete the space station because each section, or module, had to be launched one by one, then spacewalking astronauts fitted it into position. The space station has 14 modules, which makes the room inside the station about equal to the passenger cabin of a jumbo jet. If the space station landed on Earth, it would cover an entire soccer field.

- -

SIZE: 236 ft long and 354 ft wide

WEIGHT: 463 tons

CREW: 3, maximum 6

SPEED: 17,150 miles per hour

ORBITS PER DAY: 15

HEIGHT: 250 miles

COST: $7.5 million per day

- -

ORBIT

The ISS

Earth

The ISS crew arrive and leave in a three-person spacecraft, which docks to an airlock.

LIFE ON BOARD

- - - - - - - - - - - - - - -

The crews of the ISS live there for 6 months, then are replaced. While on board, the crew carries out science experiments in the three laboratories. They also help with growing vegetables to research farming in space—and get delicious greens, too! The water used for watering, drinking, and washing is recycled from the toilets and showers!

The panels that power the ISS, make the same amount of electricity as is used by 125 houses down on Earth.

ORBITS

The ISS moves very fast—about 30 times faster than a passenger plane—so it takes 93 minutes for it to fly all the way around the world. Every orbit has a dark nighttime and bright daytime lasting 45 minutes each.

The ISS is about 250 miles above the Earth, and even at that height there is a tiny bit of air outside. This air drags on the space station, making it slow down and gradually sink toward Earth. Every few months, the crew fire the space station's two rocket engines to push it back up to the correct orbit.

Bright daytime lasts 45 minutes.

Dark nighttime lasts 45 minutes.

In full sunlight, the temperature outside gets as hot as an oven. At night, the temperature drops to -238 °F. That's much colder than anywhere on Earth, even the South **Pole**.

THE MOON

The **Moon** is covered in thousands of craters and has dark patches of flat rock known as "lunar seas." While Earth orbits the Sun, the Moon orbits Earth, taking about 28 Earth days to complete one orbit. The Moon also spins around as it moves through space. It takes 28 Earth days to spin once. This means that the same side of the Moon is always facing Earth.

Most astronomers think that when Earth was young, it was hit by a planet about the size of Mars, gouging out chunks of Earth and throwing them into space. The chunks eventually joined together to form the Moon.

SIZE: 2,160 miles across (0.25 times the size of Earth)

WEIGHT: 0.01 Earths

DISTANCE FROM EARTH: 238,854 miles (30 Earth widths)

ATMOSPHERE: None

SCALE

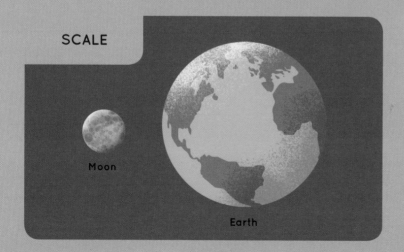

Moon

Earth

TIDES

The Moon is held in place because our planet's gravity pulls on it. However, the Moon pulls back, making Earth's oceans bulge. We see this effect as the tides that rise and fall. As the Earth spins each day, the bulge sweeps around the globe. When the bulge reaches land, the water rises up the shore. This is high tide.

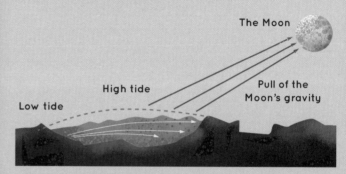

The Moon

High tide

Low tide

Pull of the Moon's gravity

The pull of the Moon's gravity gives us ocean tides.

The first two people to walk on the Moon were Neil Armstrong and Buzz Aldrin, who landed on July 20, 1969.

When astronauts landed on the near side of the Moon, they saw Earth in the sky. But if astronauts stood on the far side of the Moon (they never have done this!), it would be impossible to see Earth.

When the Moon and Sun are on opposite sides of Earth, the Sun lights up the whole of the near side of the Moon. From Earth, we see a round disc called the Full Moon. As the Moon moves around Earth, the Sun shines on different parts of it, making it appear to change shape. When the Moon and Sun are on the same side of Earth, the Sun shines on the Moon's far side, so we cannot see anything there—or perhaps just a sliver of light.

Our view of the Moon from Earth

Quarter Moon

Gibbous Moon

Crescent Moon

Sun

Full Moon

Earth

New Moon

Rocks collected from the Moon show it is made of the same materials found in Earth's mantle. This backs up the idea that the Moon was formed from broken chunks of Earth.

THE SUN

The Sun is the nearest star to Earth. It is the source of all our light and heat. Everything we see in the Solar System—the Moon and planets—is lit up for us by the Sun.

The Sun is a giant ball of plasma—a super-hot, electric gas. The ball is trying to get as small as possible, so the gas sinks to the center. The gas is made of small **particles** called **atoms**. At the Sun's center, the atoms are being squashed so much that two small atoms turn into one bigger one. As they do, they give out heat and light. It takes 100,000 years for this energy to get from the middle of the Sun to its surface. Once there, it streams into space and takes 3 minutes to reach the nearest planet: Mercury.

SIZE: 864,760 miles across (109 times bigger than Earth)

WEIGHT: 2.2 septillion tons

DISTANCE: 93 million miles from Earth

SURFACE TEMPERATURE: 9,930 °F

AGE: 4.6 billion years

SCALE

The Sun

Earth

HOT, HOT, HOTTER

The chromosphere is the coolest part of the Sun, reaching 7,770 °F. The core of the Sun is 27 million °F. The hottest part of the Sun is actually outside it, in the corona, which is the atmosphere that surrounds the Sun. It can reach a massive 36 million °F!

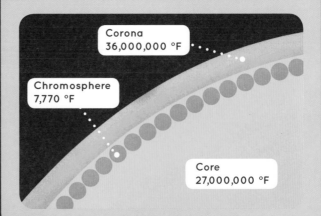

Corona
36,000,000 °F

Chromosphere
7,770 °F

Core
27,000,000 °F

It takes 8 minutes for the Sun's light and heat to reach the Earth. If the Sun went out suddenly (don't worry: it won't), we wouldn't know about it for 8 minutes!

Light

Corona

Chromosphere

Photosphere

SOLAR WIND

The Sun doesn't only release light and heat. It also releases electrified atoms, which fly off into space, forming a "solar wind." If the solar wind hit Earth directly, it would be catastrophic. Luckily, the Earth's magnetic field acts as a shield. Some wind does get through, however, and smashes into the air near the North and South Poles. This makes the air around the poles glow in bright, beautiful colors—that's an effect called an aurora.

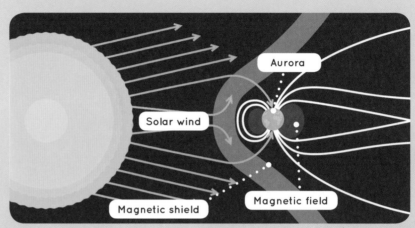

Solar wind causes an aurora at the North and South Poles.

SUN SPOTS

The Sun is covered in dark spots, called sun spots. These spots are cooler than the rest of the surface—but they are still super-hot at 6,330 °F! Sun spots appear when the Sun's magnetism gets all twisted up as it spins around. The number of sun spots goes up every few years, and then they fade away again.

The Sun takes 25 days to spin around once.

Every second, the Sun gets 4.4 million tons lighter. That is because it is turning its plasma into pure energy.

MERCURY

The closest planet to the Sun is Mercury. Like the other inner planets—Venus, Earth, and Mars—it is made of rock and metal. Since Mercury is closer to the Sun than Earth, it is a much hotter and harsher place than our planet.

It is difficult to spot Mercury in the sky. Seen from Earth, it is always close to the Sun and hidden by the glare. On just a few days a year, it is possible to spot the little planet for a few minutes when the Sun is setting or rising.

SIZE: 3,031 miles across (0.4 times the size of Earth)

WEIGHT: 0.06 Earths

DAY: 176 Earth days

YEAR: 88 Earth days

DISTANCE FROM THE SUN: 0.4 AU

SURFACE TEMPERATURE: -274 °F to 788 °F

ATMOSPHERE: None

MOONS: 0

SCALE

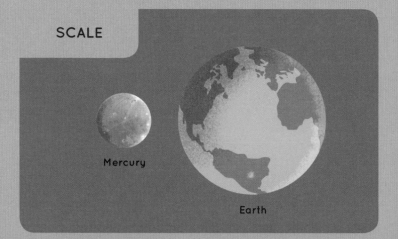

Mercury

Earth

Mercury is covered in craters made by being hit by millions of **meteorites**.

Eminescu Crater

CALORIS BASIN

The largest crater on Mercury, called the Caloris Basin, is 808 miles across. It formed when an asteroid hit Mercury about 3.9 billion years ago. The force from this impact sent a shockwave right through Mercury, which made the rock on the far side of the planet crack.

This photo taken by the *Messenger* spacecraft in 2008 uses bright colors to show different materials. The Caloris Basin is shown in orange.

Sander Crater

Munch Crater

Poe Crater

Craters on Mercury are named after artists and writers. These craters remember painter Edvard Munch, photographer August Sander, and author Edgar Allan Poe.

SPEEDY PLANET

Mercury is named after the Roman god whose job was to race around carrying messages. Mercury also travels fast, whizzing around the Sun in 88 Earth days. A rocket traveling as fast as Mercury would cross the Atlantic Ocean in 1 minute! But Mercury spins slowly on its **axis**, only once every 58 Earth days. If you were standing on Mercury, it would take 176 Earth days for the Sun to rise, set, and rise again!

Mercury was the Roman god known for his speediness—just like the planet that took his name.

Basho Crater

Some craters are surrounded by "rays" like the spokes of a wheel. These were created when meteorites smashed rocks into dust, spraying it out in all directions.

Neruda Crater

VENUS

About 100 years ago, many people believed that aliens called Venusians lived on Venus. They thought Venus was a paradise world!

Until recently, no one knew much about Venus. Even seen through telescopes, Venus is covered in yellow-white clouds. The clouds reflect sunlight, making Venus the brightest natural object in the night sky. Venus is seen before sunrise and after sunset, when it is called the Morning or Evening Star, even though it's a planet!

SIZE: 7,520 miles across (0.95 times the size of Earth)

WEIGHT: 0.8 Earths

DAY: 243 Earth days

YEAR: 224 Earth days

DISTANCE FROM THE SUN: 0.7 AU

SURFACE TEMPERATURE: 860 °F

ATMOSPHERE: Carbon dioxide, nitrogen

MOONS: 0

SCALE

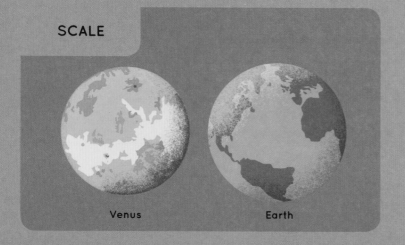

Venus   Earth

INTO THE UNKNOWN

In 1965, Russian astronomers sent *Venera 3*, an unmanned spacecraft, or 'space probe', to find out what Venus was like. *Venera 3* dropped into Venus's clouds and was never heard from again. The Russians kept sending probes. A few reached the surface but quickly broke. Finally, in 1975, *Venera 9* made it down in one piece and sent back a picture of Venus's rocky surface. In 1990–94, NASA's *Magellan* probe created maps of Venus with radar, which uses **radio waves** to bounce off the surface and build up a picture.

The *Venera 13* probe launched in 1981. It was built to be very strong to survive on Venus's surface.

The volcano Sapas Mons is 250 miles wide. Like volcanoes on Earth, its slopes were built up as super-hot lava flows hardened into rock.

The Sapas Mons volcano has two craters. Thanks to the *Magellan* probe, we have a good idea what they look like.

Venus's Atla Regio region has six large volcanoes. The largest is Maat Mons, which is 5 miles tall.

NOT A PARADISE!

Venera 9 found that Venus is the hottest planet in the Solar System. The thick, heavy atmosphere traps the Sun's heat, making it hotter than an oven! When it rains on Venus, the raindrops are pure **acid**.

Thick clouds of acid

Mist of acid and dust

The atmosphere on Venus would be deadly to humans.

MARS

Ancient people named this planet after the Roman god of war. Mars is the planet in the Solar System most similar to Earth. However, it is dry and cold, so living things cannot exist there.

Mars looks red from Earth because its rocky surface is rich with iron, which turns rusty and red. Mars's poles are covered in ice, made of frozen water and carbon dioxide. Some astronomers think that, long ago, Mars was warmer and may have been covered in seas.

SIZE: 4,220 miles across (0.5 times the size of Earth)

WEIGHT: 0.15 Earths

DAY: 24.5 Earth hours

YEAR: 687 Earth days

DISTANCE FROM THE SUN: 1.5 AU

SURFACE TEMPERATURE: -193 °F to 68 °F

ATMOSPHERE: Carbon dioxide

MOONS: 2

SCALE

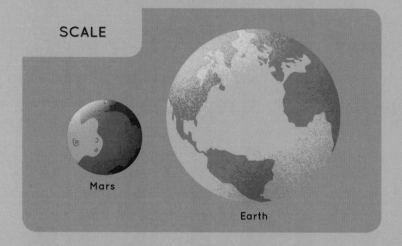

Mars

Earth

BIGGEST VOLCANO

Mars has the largest volcano (which is also the largest mountain) in the Solar System. It is called Olympus Mons and is 16.8 miles tall (nearly three times bigger than Earth's highest mountain, Mount Everest). The volcano last erupted around 25 million years ago.

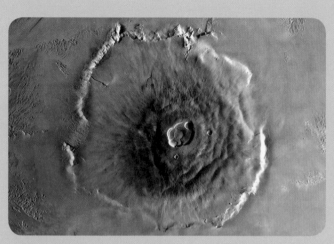

This overhead photo of Olympus Mons was taken by NASA's *Viking 1* space probe in 1978.

If simple life once existed on Mars, it would have left chemicals in the rocks. *Curiosity* has drills, brushes for collecting dust, and lasers for blasting rocks apart to test them.

MARTIAN MOONS

Mars has two small moons, named Phobos and Deimos. These are nothing like Earth's Moon: they are only about as wide as a city and look like giant boulders covered in craters. Astronomers think the moons were once asteroids that came too close to Mars and were pulled into orbit by the planet's gravity. The moons' names mean "Fear" and "Terror," who were the children of the Greek god of war, named Ares.

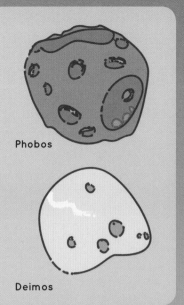

Phobos

Deimos

CURIOSITY

Since 2012, NASA's *Curiosity* rover has been rolling over Mars's surface. The rover's main job is to look for traces of water and signs of alien life. Although there is probably no life on Mars today, astronomers wonder if that was always the case.

Curiosity receives instructions from Earth using radio waves. However, if a rock or a hole blocks the rover's way, it knows how to get out of trouble on its own.

THE ASTEROID BELT

The Asteroid Belt is a ring of rocks that orbit the Sun in a large gap between the orbits of Mars and Jupiter. Astronomers have counted 50,000 large rocks that range from car-sized to country-sized, but there are probably millions of smaller rocks as well. Asteroid means "star-like."

Asteroids are made of metals and rock. Many of the metals are rare on Earth. We use them to make batteries and computer microchips. Companies are figuring out if it is possible to send mining spacecraft to these asteroids.

LARGEST ASTEROID: Ceres (590 miles across)

WEIGHT OF ALL ROCKS IN THE BELT: 0.04 Earth Moons

AVERAGE DISTANCE FROM THE SUN: 2.2–3.2 AU

AVERAGE SPEED OF ORBIT: 15 miles per second

MOONS: 143 asteroids have their own moons

LOCATION

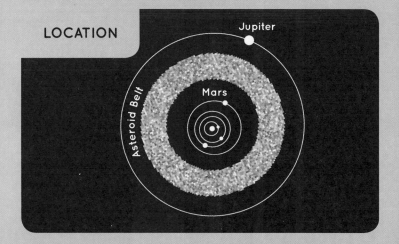

Jupiter

Mars

Asteroid Belt

DANGER TO EARTH

Thousands of asteroids orbit outside the main Asteroid Belt. Some of them come close to Earth. Asteroids do not follow simple orbits: the gravity of big planets makes the rocks swerve and loop through space. Astronomers watch the "Near-Earth Asteroids" to check if one is going to hit us. If needed, we could send spacecraft to knock the asteroid out of its collision course.

In 2013, a small Near-Earth Asteroid entered Earth's atmosphere above Chelyabinsk, Russia.

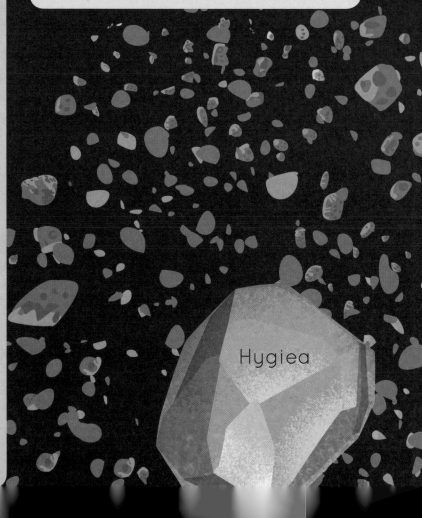

Hygiea

The first asteroid to be found was Ceres, in 1801, and it is also the biggest. If Ceres landed on Earth it would cover Spain. Ceres is so large that astronomers call it a **dwarf planet** (see page 32). About half the weight of the Asteroid Belt is contained in the four largest asteroids: Ceres, Vesta, Pallas, and Hygiea.

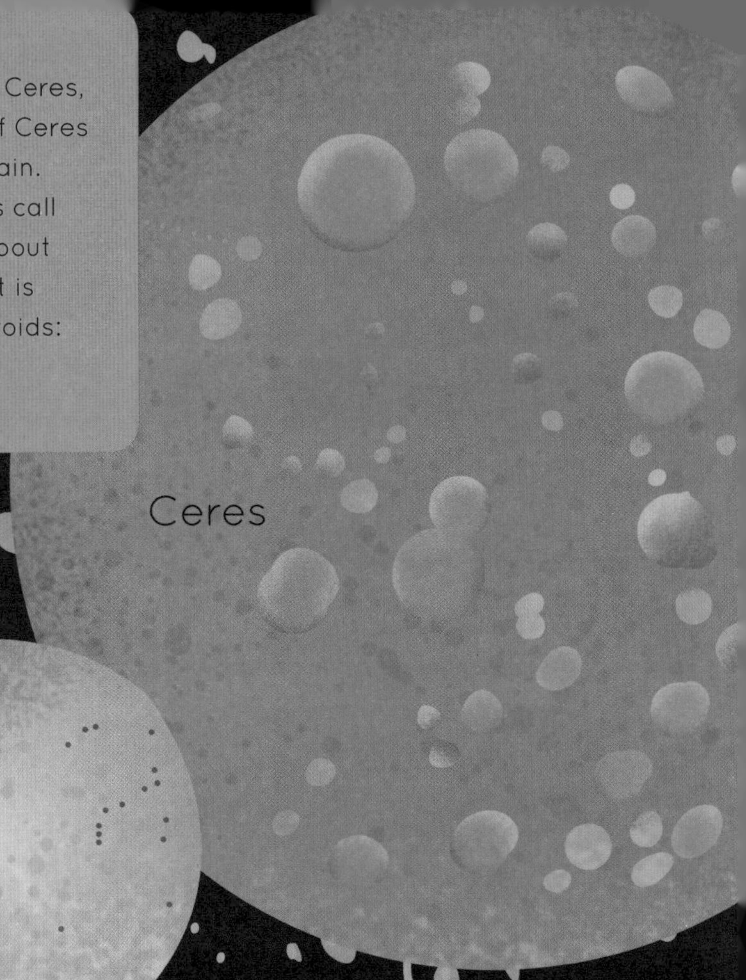

Ceres

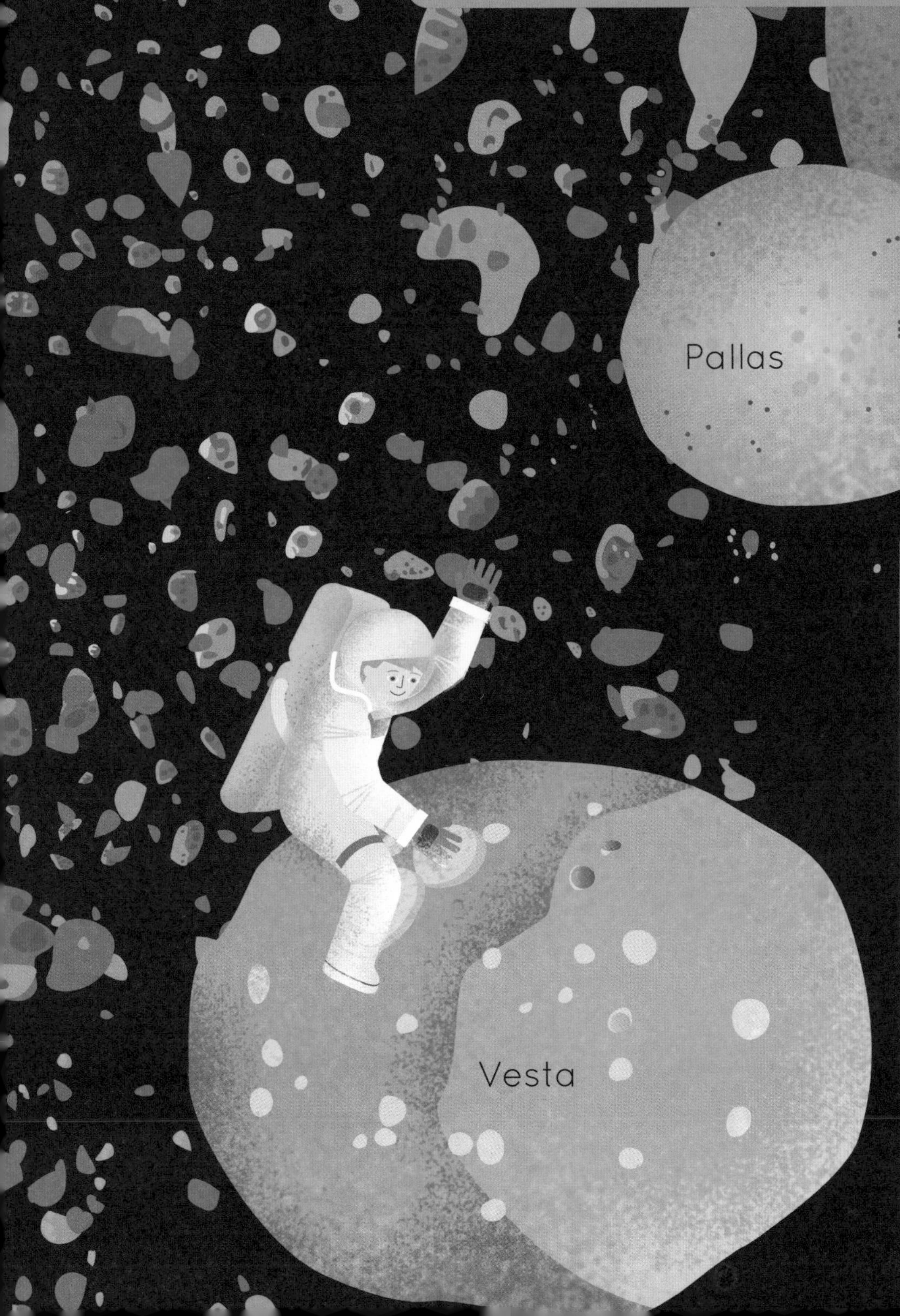

Pallas

Vesta

ASTEROID LANDER

In 2001, a space probe called *NEAR-Shoemaker* landed on a Near-Earth Asteroid named Eros. Eros is shaped like a 10-mile-long peanut. The gravity of Eros does not pull to the middle of the asteroid, but pulls toward the larger, heavier ends. That means that, in some places on Eros, things will fall uphill!

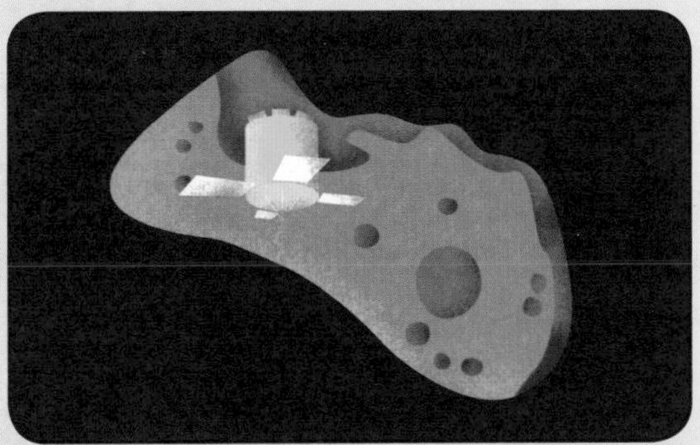

Eros was the first asteroid to be landed on.

JUPITER

Jupiter is the biggest and heaviest planet in the Solar System. It is a gas giant. Much of it is made of liquid and thick, foggy gases.

When the Sun was young, it was surrounded by dust and gases. The dust was heavier, so it was pulled nearer to the Sun, forming the inner, rocky planets: Mercury, Venus, Earth, and Mars. The gas farther away from the Sun formed the giant, gassy outer planets: Jupiter, Saturn, Uranus, and Neptune.

SIZE: 88,846 miles across (11 times the size of Earth)

WEIGHT: 318 Earths

DAY: 10 Earth hours

YEAR: 12 Earth years

DISTANCE FROM THE SUN: 5 AU

SURFACE TEMPERATURE: -148 °F

ATMOSPHERE: Hydrogen, helium, methane

MOONS: 69, plus a faint ring system

SCALE

Earth

Jupiter

JUNO TO JUPITER

NASA's *Juno* space probe went into orbit around Jupiter in 2016. *Juno*'s mission is to search for clues about the planet's core and to study its atmosphere and winds, which can reach up to 384 miles per hour.

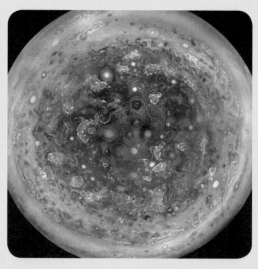

In 2017, *Juno* took this photo of storms around Jupiter's South Pole.

Jupiter has layers of liquid and gassy hydrogen and helium, around a core of rock and ice.

Jupiter's second biggest moon, Callisto, has more craters for its size than any object in the Solar System.

Jupiter's largest moon, Ganymede, is also the largest moon in the Solar System.

The third largest moon, Io, is the most volcanically active place in the Solar System.

The fourth biggest moon, Europa, has a hidden ocean of water, covered in ice. Could this ocean be home to alien life?

Jupiter's clouds tangle into vast storms. The largest, called the Great Red Spot, has been raging since at least 1665.

SATURN

This is the second largest planet in the Solar System. Like Jupiter, it is a gas giant. All the giant planets have a ring system, but Saturn has the largest and brightest.

Like the other giant planets, Saturn is made mostly from hydrogen and helium, which are the lightest materials in the Universe. Helium is the gas in party balloons. Saturn is the most lightweight planet. If it were possible to put Saturn in a giant bucket of water, it would float.

· ·

SIZE: 74,898 miles across (9.5 times the size of Earth)

WEIGHT: 95 Earths

DAY: 10.5 Earth hours

YEAR: 29 Earth years

DISTANCE FROM THE SUN: 9.5 AU

SURFACE TEMPERATURE: -220 °F

ATMOSPHERE: Hydrogen, helium, methane

MOONS: 62, plus a ring system

· ·

SCALE

Earth

Saturn

Saturn's main rings stretch from 4,000 to 50,000 miles away from Saturn's **equator**. They are made of billions of pieces of ice that range from tiny specks to chunks as big as a house. Although Saturn's rings are massively wide, they are only about 30 feet thick.

TITAN

Saturn's largest moon is Titan. Like Jupiter's moon Ganymede, it is larger than Mercury. It is the only moon in the Solar System with a thick atmosphere, which forms orange clouds. In 2004, a landing craft named *Huygens* was dropped onto Titan by the *Cassini* probe. It found that the moon was covered in lakes and rivers, but instead of water, they were filled with gasoline-like liquids!

This photograph taken by *Cassini* shows Titan behind Saturn's rings and the smaller moon Epimetheus.

Saturn is not a perfect ball shape. It is flattened at the poles and bulges at the equator.

THE CASSINI MISSION

The *Cassini* space probe spent 13 years studying Saturn. It was named after Italian astronomer Giovanni Cassini, who correctly suggested in 1675 that Saturn's "ring" was actually several rings, with gaps between them. In 2017, *Cassini* made one final mission, flying straight into Saturn's atmosphere. The spacecraft sent back information about the chemicals in the clouds before it was ripped apart.

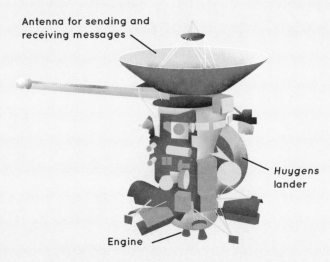

Antenna for sending and receiving messages

Huygens lander

Engine

Cassini went into orbit around Saturn in 2004.

URANUS

Uranus can just be spotted in the night sky without a telescope, but it is so dim that it was mistaken for a star until 1781.

Uranus is an ice giant, like the next planet in the Solar System, Neptune. They are both made of the same kind of material as Jupiter and Saturn, but they are much farther from the Sun and much colder. Instead of being giant balls of gas, the outer two planets are giant balls of ice, liquid, and extremely cold gas.

SIZE: 31,763 miles across (4 times the size of Earth)

WEIGHT: 15 Earths

DAY: 17 Earth hours and 14 minutes

YEAR: 84 Earth years

DISTANCE FROM THE SUN: 19 AU

SURFACE TEMPERATURE: -328 °F

ATMOSPHERE: Hydrogen, helium, methane

MOONS: 27, plus a ring system

SCALE

Earth

Uranus

BIG RINGS

Little was known about Uranus until the 1980s, when the *Voyager 2* probe flew by. It revealed the huge size of Uranus's rings: the outer ring, number 13, stretches 61,000 miles from the planet. The rings are made mostly of ice, coated with grime.

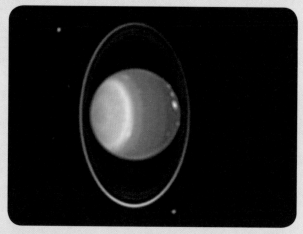

The *Hubble Space Telescope* took this photo of Uranus, its rings, and some of its moons.

White clouds can be seen in Uranus's atmosphere.

IT'S A PLANET!

In 1781, Uranus became the first planet to be discovered with a telescope. Using a telescope he built himself, the astonomer William Herschel noticed the distant "star" was actually orbiting the Sun like a planet.

The discovery of Uranus made Herschel famous.

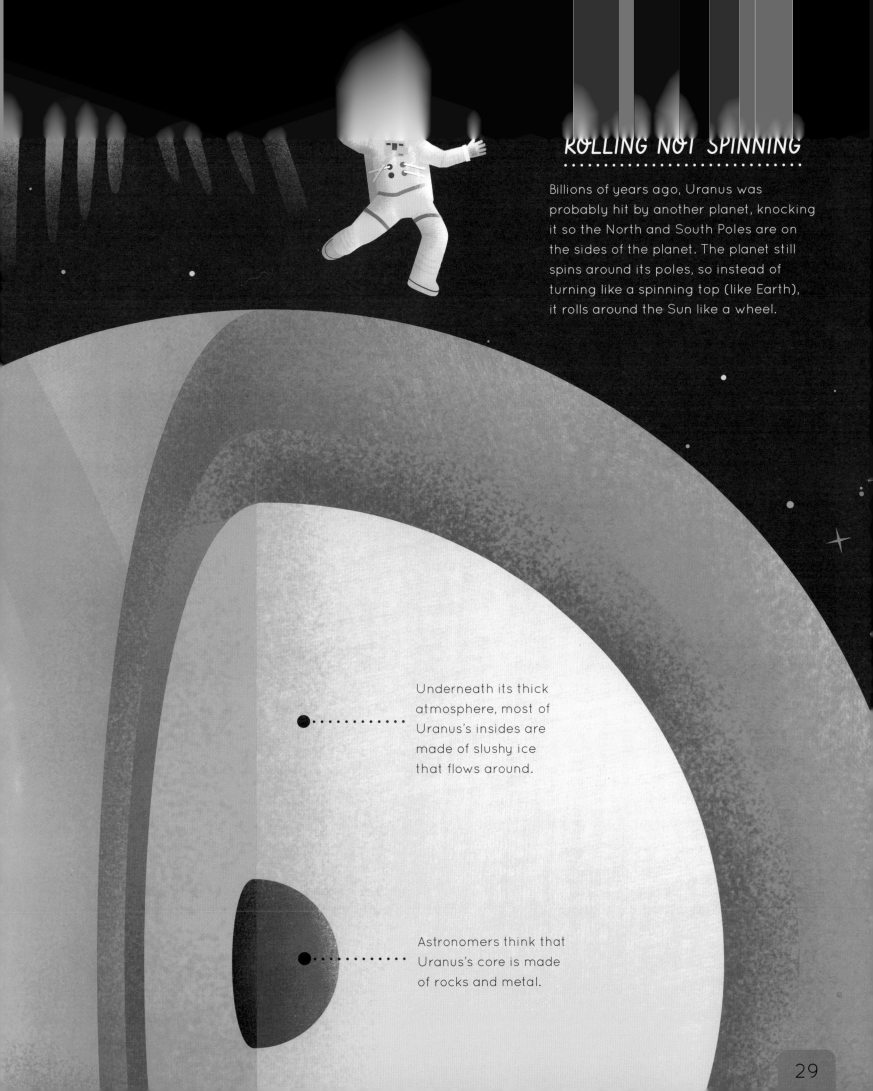

ROLLING NOT SPINNING

Billions of years ago, Uranus was probably hit by another planet, knocking it so the North and South Poles are on the sides of the planet. The planet still spins around its poles, so instead of turning like a spinning top (like Earth), it rolls around the Sun like a wheel.

Underneath its thick atmosphere, most of Uranus's insides are made of slushy ice that flows around.

Astronomers think that Uranus's core is made of rocks and metal.

NEPTUNE

Neptune has a deep blue color as if it is covered in water, so its discoverers named it after the Roman god of the sea. In fact, Neptune is an ice giant, made mostly of slushy ice. Like Uranus, it probably has a core of rock.

Neptune has the wildest weather in the Solar System. The planet's winds blow at 1,250 miles per hour, 20 times faster than a hurricane on Earth. White clouds called scooters are blown right around the planet.

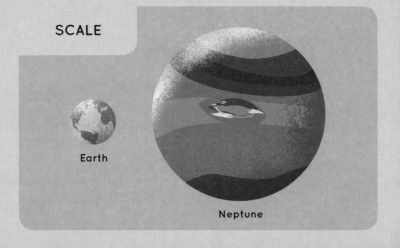

SIZE: 30,775 miles across (3.8 times the size of Earth)

WEIGHT: 17 Earths

DAY: 16 Earth hours

YEAR: 165 Earth years

DISTANCE FROM THE SUN: 30 AU

SURFACE TEMPERATURE: -328 °F

ATMOSPHERE: Hydrogen, helium, methane

MOONS: 14, plus a faint ring system

SCALE

Earth

Neptune

WHY THE WOBBLE?

After figuring out Uranus's path around the Sun, astronomers saw that it wobbles a little. This showed that another, more distant planet was pulling on it. This realization led to the discovery of Neptune in 1846.

GREAT DARK SPOT

Voyager 2 passed Neptune in 1989, capturing images of a 8,000-mile storm that was soon named the Great Dark Spot. Five years later, when the *Hubble Telescope* photographed Neptune, the storm had disappeared, but a new, huge storm had appeared.

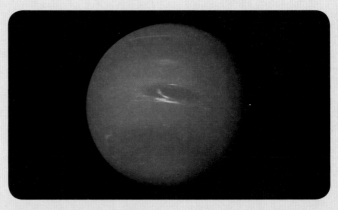

Voyager 2 took this photo of Neptune when it passed 4 million miles from the planet. The Great Dark Spot can be seen at the center.

Neptune's clouds look a bit like Earth's clouds, but they are made of methane ice crystals rather than water.

Neptune has at least five rings. They are made of icy boulders, darkened by a coating of grime.

WRONG WAY, TRITON!

Neptune's largest moon is Triton. All other moons in the Solar System orbit their planet in the same direction as the planet spins. But Triton orbits Neptune in the opposite direction. That suggests that Triton comes from the outer Solar System and was captured by Neptune's gravity, becoming its moon.

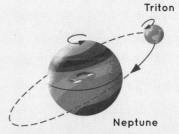

Triton spins in the opposite direction from Neptune.

PLUTO

In 1930, Clyde Tombaugh discovered Pluto. It was thought that Pluto was bigger than Earth, so it was named the ninth planet in the Solar System. Pluto is so far away it took years to figure out that it is actually smaller than our Moon. In 2006, astronomers decided Pluto should be described as a dwarf planet.

Pluto is the largest object in the Kuiper Belt, a distant region of the Solar System where icy objects swing around the Sun.

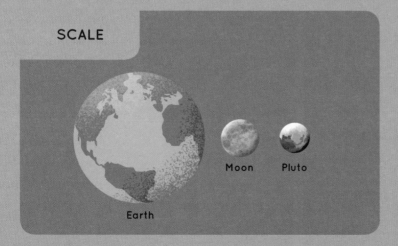

SIZE: 1,413 miles across (0.18 times the size of Earth)

WEIGHT: 0.002 Earths

DAY: 6 Earth days

YEAR: 248 Earth years

DISTANCE FROM THE SUN: 39 AU

SURFACE TEMPERATURE: -380 °F

ATMOSPHERE: Nitrogen, methane, carbon monoxide

MOONS: 5

SCALE

Earth

Moon

Pluto

WHAT IS A DWARF PLANET?

A dwarf planet is an object that orbits the Sun. (Unlike a moon, which orbits a planet.) A dwarf planet is large enough for the pull of its own gravity to crush it into a ball-like planet shape. However, unlike a true planet, a dwarf planet's gravity is not strong enough to clear its orbit, so its path is crossed by other objects. At the time of writing, astronomers agree there are five other dwarf planets in our Solar System: Ceres, in the Asteroid Belt (see page 23); and Eris, Haumea, Makemake, and Sedna, which are ice balls orbiting far beyond Neptune. Astronomers are likely to find more dwarf planets in the future.

Eris

Haumea

Makemake

Sedna

Styx

Hydra

The dwarf planet Pluto is named after the Greek and Roman god of the dead, Pluto.

NEW HORIZONS

In 2006, the *New Horizons* space probe was sent to study Pluto. It took more than nine years to get there, arriving during Pluto's long summer. (In the winter, it gets so cold that Pluto's atmosphere freezes solid.) The probe saw that Pluto's surface is made mostly of frozen nitrogen.

In this image taken by *New Horizons*, the large pale area on Pluto's surface is an ice sheet named Tombaugh Regio.

Pluto

Charon

Nix

PLUTO'S MOONS

The largest of Pluto's moons, Charon, is named after the boatman who brings the dead to the underworld in Greek myths. The moon orbits so close that Charon and Pluto swing around each other. The other moons are also named after creatures and places in the Greek underworld.

Kerberos

HALLEY'S COMET

The nucleus of a comet is made of rock, dust, and ice.

When a comet gets closer to the Sun, it heats up. A glowing cloud of gas and dust, called a coma, surrounds the nucleus, making the comet much brighter.

A comet is an amazing sight as its streaks across the sky with a long, bright tail. Comet means "long-haired" in Greek. Comets only come close to Earth a few times each century, but there are thousands dashing through the Solar System. A few comets get so bright we see them during the day—that's amazing as they are just giant space snowballs!

The most famous comet is Halley's Comet, named after the English astronomer Edmond Halley. In 1705, Halley calculated that the comet seen in 1682 would return in 1759. He was correct: Halley's Comet passes close to Earth every 76 years or so.

SIZE: 9 miles long and 5 miles wide

WEIGHT: 242 trillion tons

ORBIT: 74-79 Earth years

FIRST RECORDED: 240 BCE

LAST VISIT: 1986

NEXT VISIT: 2061

ORBIT

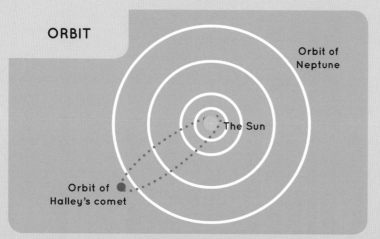

Orbit of Neptune

The Sun

Orbit of Halley's comet

As a comet nears the Sun, gases in the nucleus are electrified by the sunlight, forming a tail.

METEOR SHOWERS

Comets leave a trail of dust. When Earth passes through the trail, the dust burns up in our atmosphere, making meteor showers. During a shower, there are hundreds of streaks of light, often called shooting stars.

The best shower to look for, called the Perseids, is in August. It is caused by dust from the Swift-Tuttle Comet.

LANDING ON A COMET

In 2014, the *Rosetta* space probe met up with comet 67P/Churyumov-Gerasimenko (67P for short). *Rosetta* sent *Philae*, a lander about the size of a washing machine, to the comet's surface to see what it was made of. *Rosetta* orbited 67P for two years, watching as it sprouted its tail.

Rosetta took this photo of 67P from 17 miles away.

A jet of dust bursts from the nucleus, making a brighter tail that shoots off at a different angle. The longest comet tails reach 300 million miles.

PROXIMA CENTAURI

Beyond the Solar System, there are no planets, asteroids, or comets for billions, or even trillions, of miles. If a spacecraft could travel as fast as a beam of light, it would travel through this emptiness for more than four years before reaching the nearest star—Proxima Centauri (proxima means "nearest").

Proxima Centauri is part of a star system called Alpha Centauri. A star system is a small number of stars that orbit each other. Alpha Centauri contains three stars: Alpha Centauri A and B, and Proxima Centauri, which is about 560 billion miles closer than the other two.

SIZE: 0.15 times the Sun

AGE: 4.9 billion years

BRIGHTNESS: 0.001 Suns

LIFETIME: 200 billion years

STAR TYPE: Red dwarf

DISTANCE FROM THE SUN:
4.2 light-years

SCALE

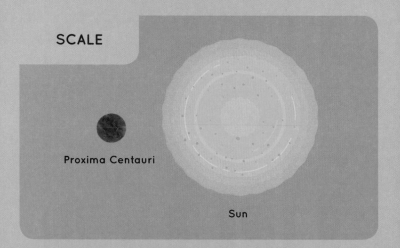

Proxima Centauri

Sun

THE VIEW FROM EARTH

The Alpha Centauri star system is in the constellation Centaurus. From Earth, it is very bright. This is partly because it is close to Earth, but also due to the light coming not from one star, but three. Without a telescope, the three stars look like one star.

In this photo, the Alpha Centauri star system is the bright yellowish "star" at the bottom right. It is pictured from La Silla Observatory in Chile.

Alpha Centauri B is slightly smaller and cooler than its partner, Alpha Centauri A.

Proxima Centauri spins around the bigger two stars at a distance of 13,000 AU.

DWARF STARS

All the stars in the Alpha Centauri system are dwarf stars. Most stars are dwarfs, including our Sun. Astronomers divide stars into two main types: dwarfs and giants. Dwarfs are smaller and less bright than giants, but they shine for longer. The color of light from a star tells astronomers how large and hot it is. Alpha Centauri A is a yellow dwarf (a medium-hot star like our Sun); Alpha Centauri B is a cooler orange dwarf; and Proxima Centauri is a red dwarf, the smallest and coolest type.

Red dwarfs like Proxima Centauri are the most common stars.

Alpha Centauri A is spinning around with a slightly smaller partner, Alpha Centauri B. The pair are spinning round a common center: a point in space between the two stars.

EXOPLANET PROXIMA B

Until the end of the 20th century, some people thought our Sun might be the only star in the Universe surrounded by orbiting planets. Today, astronomers have discovered thousands of exoplanets—planets that orbit other stars. They think more than half of stars have at least two planets. That means there are more planets in the Universe than stars!

There are even planets in the Alpha Centauri star system. One of them is exoplanet Proxima Centauri b ("Proxima b" for short), which is in orbit around our closest star, Proxima Centauri. This makes it the closest known exoplanet.

SIZE: 0.8–1.5 times the size of Earth

WEIGHT: 1.3 to 3 times the weight of Earth

YEAR: 11 Earth days

DISTANCE FROM ITS STAR: 0.05 AU

DISTANCE FROM THE SUN: 4.2 light-years

SCALE

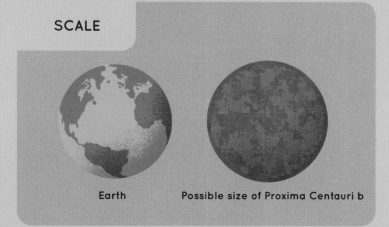

Earth   Possible size of Proxima Centauri b

On the exoplanet Proxima Centauri b, the star Proxima Centauri warms the planet like the Sun warms Earth.

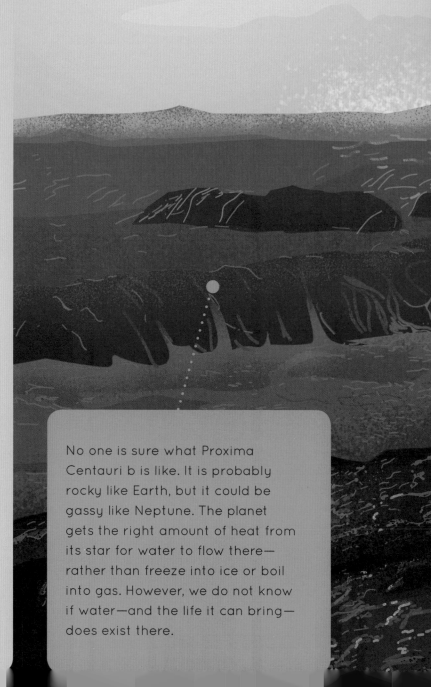

No one is sure what Proxima Centauri b is like. It is probably rocky like Earth, but it could be gassy like Neptune. The planet gets the right amount of heat from its star for water to flow there—rather than freeze into ice or boil into gas. However, we do not know if water—and the life it can bring—does exist there.

The stars Alpha Centauri A and Alpha Centauri B shine more weakly on the planet.

NEW WORLDS

At the moment, astronomers only really know how heavy each exoplanet is and how far away it is from its star. Even so, they have discovered that other solar systems have planets that are very different from ours. Here are just a few of the planet types:

A brown dwarf is a vast ball of gas more like a small star than a planet. However, it is not big and hot enough to shine like a star.

An Earthlike planet is rocky with flowing water on its surface. So far, no Earthlike exoplanets have been found...

A super-Jupiter is a gas planet up to 7 times larger and 20 times heavier than Jupiter.

A rogue planet is a planet that has escaped from its solar system and is floating through interstellar space.

An exomoon is the moon of an exoplanet. Only a handful of possible exomoons have been found.

ESKIMO NEBULA

Dwarf stars last for billions of years, but they do not last forever. Our own Sun has about 6 billion years of life left. To see what happens when a dwarf star dies, we need to travel to a gas cloud called the Eskimo **Nebula**. This colorful cloud formed when a star like the Sun started to die.

The Eskimo Nebula was discovered by William Herschel in 1787. Nebula means "cloud" in Latin. The nebula was given the name "Eskimo" because its rounded shells look like a head in a fur hood (although, today, we don't usually use the word "Eskimo" to describe Arctic peoples). The Eskimo Nebula is a planetary nebula, which is a confusing name as these clouds of gas have nothing to do with planets!

SIZE: 0.7 light-years across

AGE: 10,000 years

TYPE: Planetary nebula

DISTANCE FROM THE SUN: 2,870 light-years

LOCATION

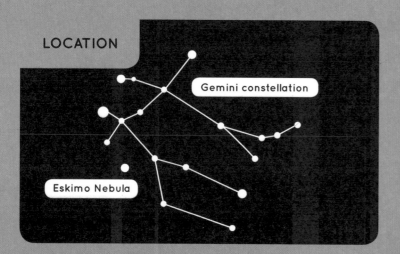

Gemini constellation

Eskimo Nebula

These fur-like wisps are about a light-year long. They are being blasted outward by a wind of gases coming from the star.

BEAUTIFUL PICTURES

Space telescopes allow astronomers to take amazing photos of planetary nebulas and other distant objects. Space telescopes orbit in space, outside the Earth's atmosphere, where their images are not spoiled by pollution and city lights. Their cameras can pick up energy waves that would be blocked by the Earth's atmosphere.

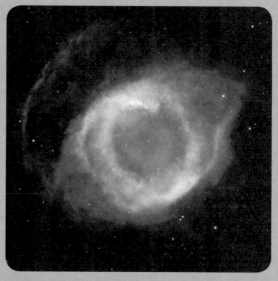

The *Hubble Space Telescope* was launched in 1990. It took this photo of the Helix Nebula in 2003.

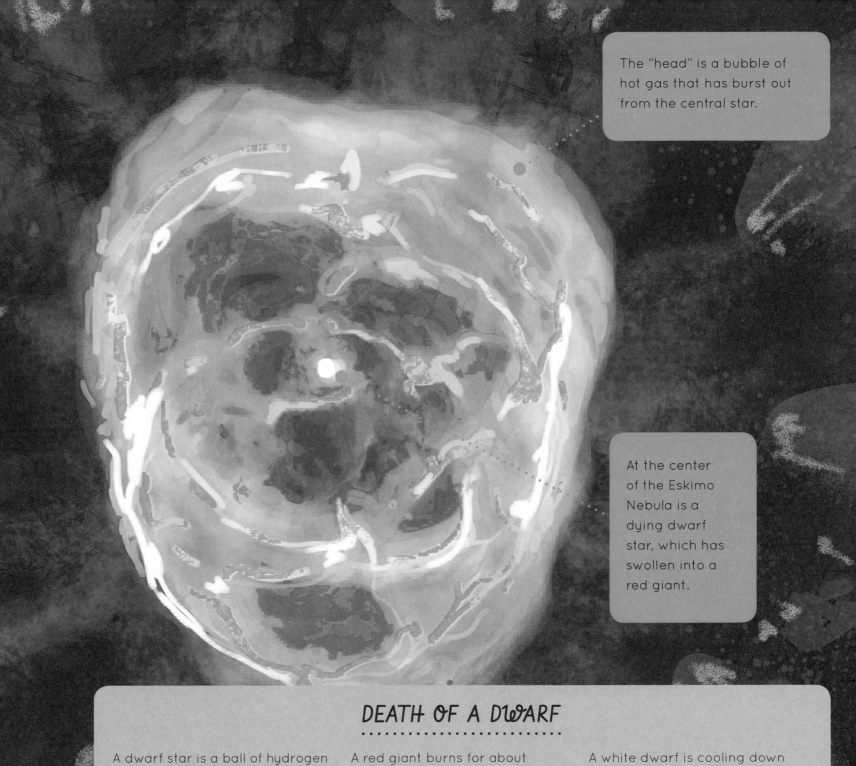

The "head" is a bubble of hot gas that has burst out from the central star.

At the center of the Eskimo Nebula is a dying dwarf star, which has swollen into a red giant.

DEATH OF A DWARF

A dwarf star is a ball of hydrogen gas. It uses hydrogen to give out heat and light by turning it into helium, a heavier gas. When the star runs out of hydrogen, it uses the helium instead. This makes the star swell into a "red giant."

A red giant burns for about 500 million years. Then the star starts to break up, blasting gas into space to create a planetary nebula. Eventually, all that is left of the dying star is a tiny hot object called a white dwarf.

A white dwarf is cooling down and will eventually stop giving out heat and light. But no white dwarf has cooled down to this point yet. It would take a million billion years and the Universe is only 13.8 billion years old!

Dwarf star

Red giant

Planetary nebula

White dwarf

VY CANIS MAJORIS

It is hard to imagine just how huge the Sun is compared to Earth. However, the Sun is tiny compared to the biggest stars. VY Canis Majoris is a red **hypergiant**, one of the largest stars of all. It gives out the same amount of light as 250,000 Suns. However, the star is nearly 4,000 light-years away, which means it is too faint to see without a telescope.

If we could bring VY Canis Majoris to our Solar System and replace the Sun with it, the star would swallow up all the rocky planets, the Asteroid Belt, and even Jupiter. Saturn would become the first planet.

- -

SIZE: 1,420 times the Sun

AGE: Less than 10 million years

BRIGHTNESS: 250,000 Suns

LIFETIME: About 10 million years

STAR TYPE: Red hypergiant

DISTANCE FROM THE SUN:
3,816 light-years

- -

LOCATION

Sirius

VY Canis Majoris

Canis Major constellation

The Sun is a yellow dwarf star.

864,000 miles across

ORION THE HUNTER

The constellation Orion is one of the easiest to spot. It is named after a hunter in Greek myths. Orion is next door to the constellations Canis Major (Bigger Dog) and Canis Minor (Smaller Dog), two of the hunter's dogs.

Betelgeuse

Orion's belt

This photo shows the constellation Orion, with the red supergiant Betelgeuse forming one of the hunter's shoulders. Orion's "belt" is made by the three stars in a line at the center. His feet are the two bright stars near the bottom.

Sirius is the brightest star in the sky as seen from Earth. It is a white star that is nearly twice as big as the Sun but 25 times brighter. Sirius is also called the Dog Star because it is part of the constellation Canis Major, meaning "Bigger Dog."

1.48 million miles across

1 billion miles across

38 million miles across

Aldebaran is a red giant that is 44 times wider than the Sun. It is about 65 light-years away and is the brightest star in the constellation of Taurus.

1.23 billion miles across

Betelgeuse, pronounced "beetle-juice," is the brightest star in the Orion constellation. It is a red supergiant, more than 1,000 times wider than the Sun. Astronomers believe Betelgeuse will explode within the next 100,000 years!

At 1,420 times the size of the Sun, VY Canis Majoris is a red hypergiant. Fewer than one in 100,000 stars are this big. VY Canis Majoris is in the Canis Major constellation.

CRAB NEBULA

When they die, giant stars do not fade away in pretty clouds of gas like smaller stars (see pages 40–41). Instead, they die in the largest explosions ever seen. The explosions are so bright that stars that were once too dim to be seen from Earth suddenly appear in our sky as a bright flash known as a supernova. It takes the Sun 10 million years to give out the same amount of light that comes from a supernova all at once.

In 1054, Chinese astronomers made notes about a "guest star" appearing in the sky. Today, astronomers think this was a supernova. The supernova's light faded away 642 days later but left behind a vast twisted cloud known as the Crab Nebula.

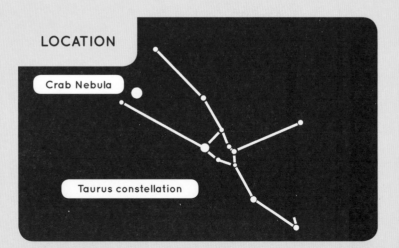

SIZE: 5.5 light-years across

AGE: Approximately 950 years

TYPE: Supernova remnant

DISTANCE FROM THE SUN: 6,500 light-years

LOCATION

Crab Nebula

Taurus constellation

CHANDRA X-RAY OBSERVATORY

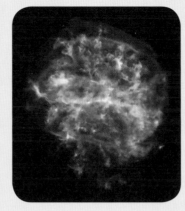

This *Chandra* image shows supernova remnant G292.0+1.8.

NASA's *Chandra X-ray Observatory* was launched into space in 1999. Its instruments pick up X-rays from super-hot parts of the Universe, such as exploding stars. X-rays are a type of energy that is invisible to humans.

The Crab Nebula is a cloud of gas and dust that is now too faint to see without a telescope. However, it is about a sixth of the size of the Moon when seen from Earth. In fact, it is more than twice as big as the entire Solar System.

At the center of the Crab Nebula is a **neutron** star. This is the remains of the giant star that exploded in a supernova 950 years ago. A neutron star weighs more than the Sun but is only 12 miles wide.

The bright, dusty "threads" of the nebula are around 27,000 °F.

HOW A SUPERNOVA HAPPENS

Any star that is more than 1.5 times heavier than the Sun will end with a supernova. When it runs out of fuel, the weight of the dead star is so great that it collapses in on itself. This crushes everything in the star's core, giving out a great flash of energy. What is left behind is usually a tiny object called a neutron star. But the very biggest stars turn into something else—a black hole (see pages 52–53).

| Small or medium star | Swells into red giant | Creates a planetary nebula | Becomes a white dwarf |

| Large star | Swells into red supergiant | Explodes as a supernova | Large stars become a neutron star / Massive stars become a black hole |

When they run out of fuel, different sized stars die in different ways.

PULSAR LGM-1

Pulsars are a type of neutron star. These are small but heavy stars that are made inside a supernova explosion when a giant star dies. All pulsars are neutron stars, but not all neutron stars are pulsars! Pulsars are neutron stars that rotate while sending out pulses of energy.

In 1967, LGM-1 was the first pulsar to be discovered, by Jocelyn Bell Burnell and Antony Hewish. When they picked up a radio signal that beeped every 1.3 seconds, they joked it might be coming from aliens—or "little green men." When they figured out the source of the energy was a pulsar, they named it LGM, short for "little green men"!

SIZE: 12 miles across

AGE: 16 million years

WEIGHT: 1.4 Suns

ROTATION: One spin every 1.3 seconds

DISTANCE FROM THE SUN: 1,000 light-years

LOCATION

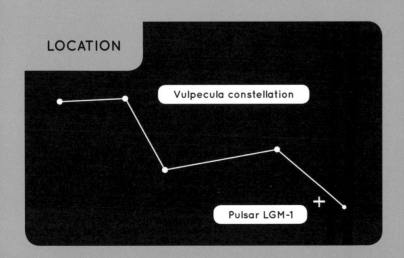

Vulpecula constellation

Pulsar LGM-1

A pulsar has a very strong magnetic field. (Like a giant magnet, Earth has a magnetic field, too.) The magnetic field channels energy into two jets, at the star's magnetic North and South Poles.

SPINNING STAR

A pulsar is like a lighthouse in space—it fires out a powerful beam of radio waves. Every time the star spins around, we can pick up the beam as it points at us. LGM-1 is a star that rotates every 1.3 seconds, which is why we can pick up its radio signal every 1.3 seconds. Radio waves are an invisible type of radiation, or energy.

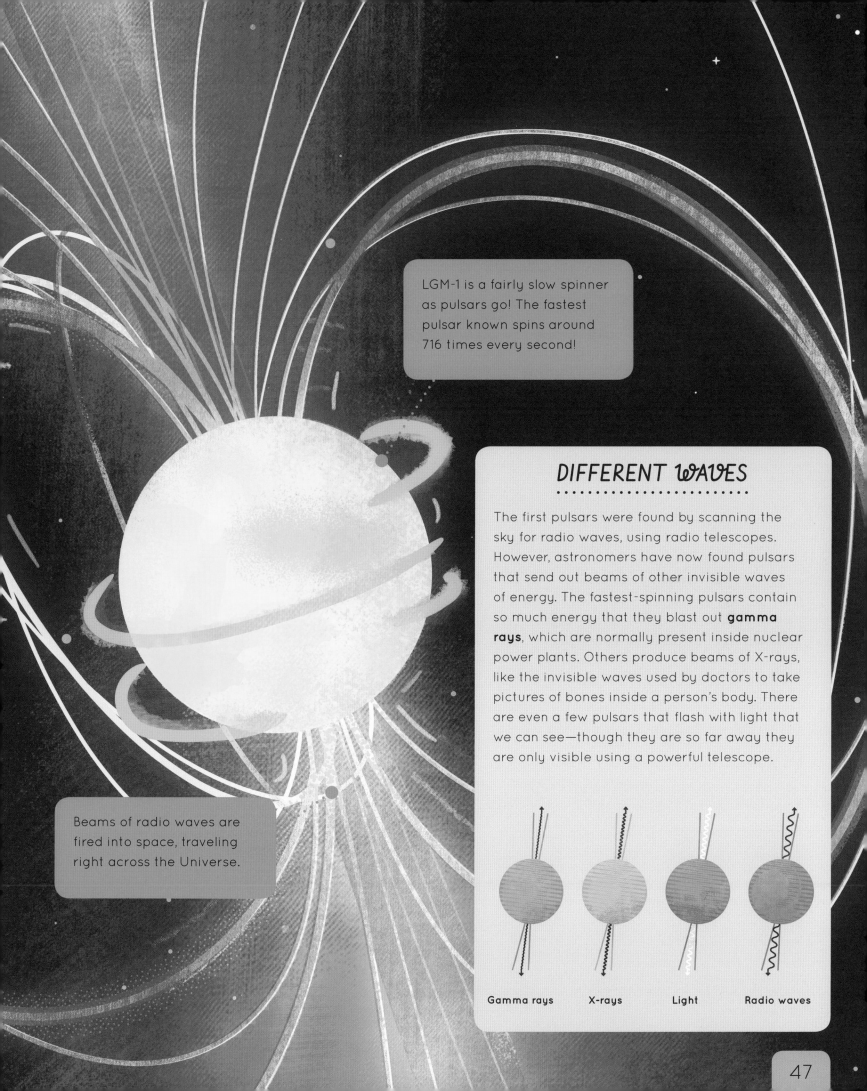

LGM-1 is a fairly slow spinner as pulsars go! The fastest pulsar known spins around 716 times every second!

Beams of radio waves are fired into space, traveling right across the Universe.

DIFFERENT WAVES

The first pulsars were found by scanning the sky for radio waves, using radio telescopes. However, astronomers have now found pulsars that send out beams of other invisible waves of energy. The fastest-spinning pulsars contain so much energy that they blast out **gamma rays**, which are normally present inside nuclear power plants. Others produce beams of X-rays, like the invisible waves used by doctors to take pictures of bones inside a person's body. There are even a few pulsars that flash with light that we can see—though they are so far away they are only visible using a powerful telescope.

Gamma rays   X-rays   Light   Radio waves

CARINA NEBULA

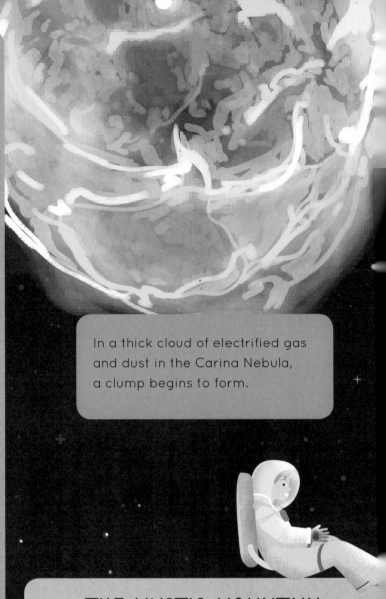

A nebula is not just the place where a star dies—it is where stars are born as well. The Carina Nebula is one of these star-making nebulas. It is 10,000 light-years away from Earth, but is so enormous that it fills a patch of sky four times bigger than a Full Moon. Different parts of this immense cloud of gas and dust have been given imaginative names by astronomers, such as the Mystic Mountain and the Caterpillar **Globule**!

The Carina Nebula is only visible from the Southern **Hemisphere**, where the nebula is bright enough to see cloudy smudges of gas and bright clusters of stars without a telescope. Astronomers study the distant nebula to learn about how stars are made.

In a thick cloud of electrified gas and dust in the Carina Nebula, a clump begins to form.

SIZE: 460 light-years across

AGE: Approximately 3 million years

TYPE: Star-forming nebula

DISTANCE FROM THE SUN: 10,000 light-years

THE MYSTIC MOUNTAIN

Near the center of the Carina Nebula is the Mystic Mountain. This is a pointed cloud 3 light-years long. Inside are several young stars that are blasting out jets of gas, which will eventually blow the Mystic Mountain cloud away.

SKY WATCH

The *Hubble Space Telescope* took this photo of the Mystic Mountain in 2010.

The clump shrinks in on itself, forming a bigger and bigger ball.

Looking like a caterpillar floating in space, the Caterpillar Globule is filled with dust. As light and heat cannot shine into the dusty globule, it is one of the coldest places in the Universe. New stars are forming inside.

The Caterpillar Globule is about one light-year across.

The ball starts to spin around and warm up, sending out jets of gas from its North and South Poles. These jets blow away the surrounding cloud. The new star is surrounded by a dusty disk.

Planets form in the disk, slowly creating a new solar system. This is how our own Solar System formed, about 4.6 billion years ago.

THE MILKY WAY

So far, all the visits on our tour have been in the swirling spiral of stars, gas, and dust called the Milky Way. The Milky Way is our galaxy, home to our Solar System.

Although we can never see the whole Milky Way from our planet, we can look into its center. This appears as a strip so thick with stars that they create a pale stripe across the night sky. The ancient Chinese called it the Silver River and the Vikings called it Winter Street. The ancient Greeks said it was the Milk Circle, while the Romans preferred the Milky Way. The Greek word for milk, "*galaxias*," gave us the word "galaxy."

SIZE: 180,000 light-years across

WEIGHT: 1 trillion Suns

NUMBER OF STARS: 400 billion

AGE: 13.7 billion years

ROTATION: Spins around once every 240 million years

SKY WATCH

The Milky Way is a spiral galaxy. Its curving arms swirl out from the Galactic Center in a counterclockwise direction. The arms are made of dwarf stars that formed from gas clouds left behind by long-dead supergiant stars.

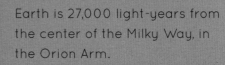

Earth is 27,000 light-years from the center of the Milky Way, in the Orion Arm.

The galaxy has a central bulge called the Galactic Center. It is filled with millions of old, bright stars.

GALAXY TYPES

All galaxies are unique, but there are three main types:

Irregular galaxy

Small, young galaxies are irregular. They may not be moving fast enough to form a spiral yet, or they may be twisted by the pull of large galaxies.

Spiral galaxy

Two-thirds of galaxies are spirals. Spirals get larger over billions of years. Older, larger galaxies pull on younger ones, creating slow-motion crashes.

Elliptical galaxy

Giant galaxies are elliptical, or egg-shaped. They are made when spiral galaxies have joined together. The largest have over 100 trillion stars.

SAGITTARIUS A* BLACK HOLE

At the very center of our Milky Way galaxy is a strange patch of sky named Sagittarius A* (astronomers say this as "A star"). There is no light coming from Sagittarius A*, but a lot of energy such as X-rays and radio waves. Everything else is hidden inside a vast dust cloud. Recently astronomers have picked up the heat from stars inside the dust. These stars are moving at huge speeds—fast enough to go twice around Earth in just one second!

There is only one thing powerful enough to make stars move that fast: a supermassive black hole. Astronomers think that most other galaxies also have a supermassive black hole at their center. The largest supermassive black hole yet found is 10,000 times the size of the Milky Way's black hole! It is 12 billion light-years away from Earth.

SIZE: 4.6 light-years across

WEIGHT: 4 million Suns

DISTANCE FROM THE SUN:
27,000 light-years

LOCATION

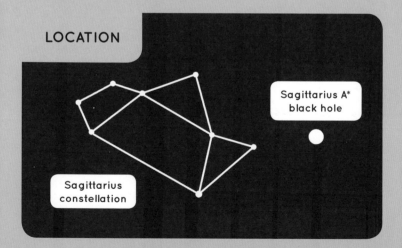

Sagittarius A*
black hole

Sagittarius
constellation

BLACK HOLES GROW

Black holes come in different sizes, from tiny to **supermassive**. Astronomers think most black holes were made when giant stars collapsed in a supernova. The crushing forces were so great that the star shrank too small to measure. This tiny dot is a black hole, but it weighs many times more than the Sun. Over time, a black hole grows as it sucks in surrounding dust and stars.

Although we cannot see Sagittarius A*, astronomers use special cameras to see the X-rays given out by dust as it is pulled into the black hole (the bright area at the center).

SWALLOWED BY A BLACK HOLE?

Could Earth be sucked into a black hole? The answer is: no! There is no black hole close enough to Earth to suck us in. The Sun will never become a black hole because it is too small to explode as a supernova.

Luckily, the Earth will never be swallowed by a black hole.

Since they are so small but so heavy, black holes produce the most powerful gravity in the Universe. Nothing can escape the pull of a black hole's gravity, not even light—which is why a black hole is black!

A black hole is surrounded by a circle called the **event horizon**. Inside this circle, the black hole will pull you in. Sagittarius A*'s event horizon is 8 million miles wide. Today, the black hole is quiet as there is nothing left within the event horizon to be pulled inside.

THE LOCAL GROUP

f we could travel inside the fastest spacecraft ever built (moving at about 10 miles per second), how long would it take to fly across the Milky Way? Nearly 2 billion years! So it is very unlikely that humans can ever leave our galaxy. However, galaxies are not the largest things in space. The Universe just keeps on building bigger and bigger.

Galaxies are not spread out evenly through the Universe—they cluster together. The Milky Way is part of a galaxy cluster named the Local Group. The Local Group contains 54 galaxies and other smaller star clusters. While gravity makes galaxies form clusters, it also makes galaxy clusters form superclusters. Along with about 100 other galaxy clusters, the Local Group is in the Virgo Supercluster.

SIZE: 10 million light-years across

NUMBER OF GALAXIES: 54

PART OF: Virgo Supercluster (110 million light-years across, with 47,000 galaxies)

LOCATION

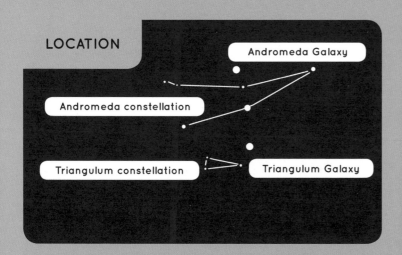

Andromeda Galaxy

Andromeda constellation

Triangulum constellation

Triangulum Galaxy

The Local Group is held together by gravity, with the small galaxies orbiting the big ones. The Large Magellanic Cloud is probably the largest galaxy orbiting the Milky Way.

Leo II

Ursa Minor

Draco

Milky Way

Large Magellanic Cloud

Small Magellanic Cloud

Sculptor

Fornax

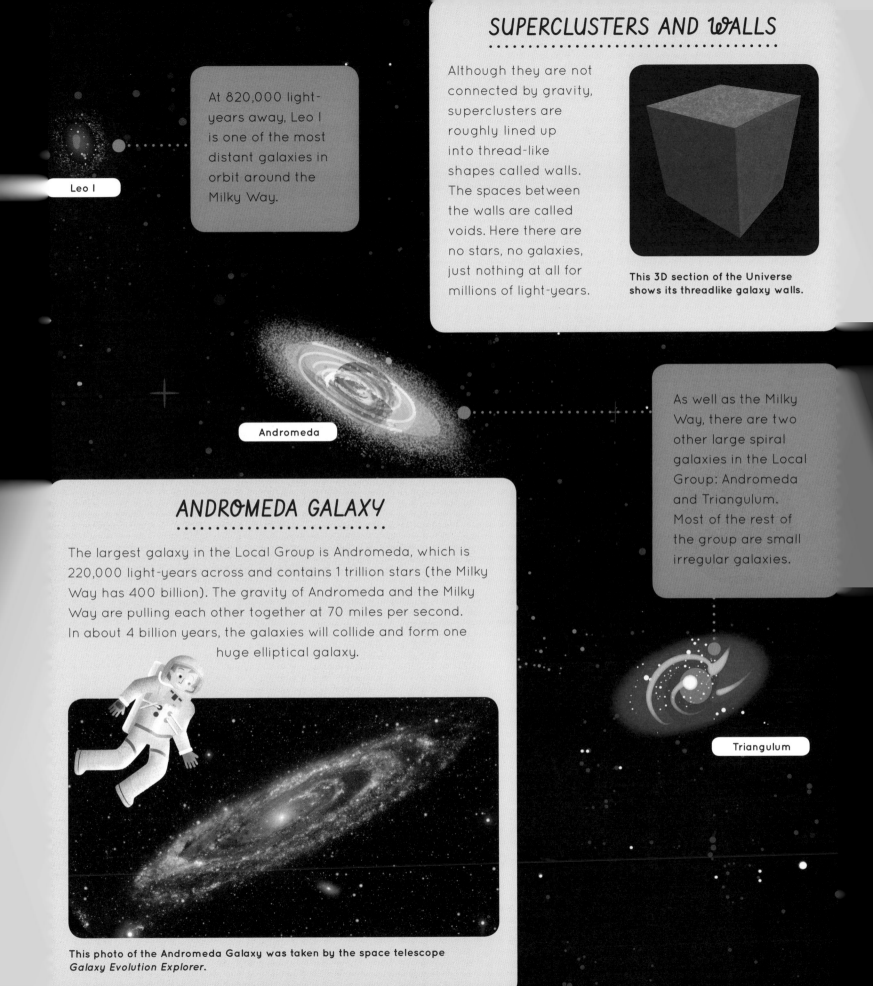

At 820,000 light-years away, Leo I is one of the most distant galaxies in orbit around the Milky Way.

Leo I

SUPERCLUSTERS AND WALLS

Although they are not connected by gravity, superclusters are roughly lined up into thread-like shapes called walls. The spaces between the walls are called voids. Here there are no stars, no galaxies, just nothing at all for millions of light-years.

This 3D section of the Universe shows its threadlike galaxy walls.

Andromeda

As well as the Milky Way, there are two other large spiral galaxies in the Local Group: Andromeda and Triangulum. Most of the rest of the group are small irregular galaxies.

ANDROMEDA GALAXY

The largest galaxy in the Local Group is Andromeda, which is 220,000 light-years across and contains 1 trillion stars (the Milky Way has 400 billion). The gravity of Andromeda and the Milky Way are pulling each other together at 70 miles per second. In about 4 billion years, the galaxies will collide and form one huge elliptical galaxy.

Triangulum

This photo of the Andromeda Galaxy was taken by the space telescope *Galaxy Evolution Explorer*.

QUASAR 3C 273

The black hole at the center of the Milky Way is fairly calm, because it has run out of nearby stars to eat. This is because the Milky Way and its black hole have been around for 13 billion years. Young galaxies have very active black holes at their center, eating up thousands of stars. We call these intensely bright galaxies **quasars** (short for "quasi-stellar radio source").

All quasars are a very long way from Earth. Quasar 3C 273 is one of the closest, but it is about 2 billion light-years away. Its light has taken so long to reach us that we are seeing the galaxy as it was 2 billion years ago. This is why all quasars are so far away—the farther away an object is, the younger it looks to us.

DISTANCE FROM THE SUN:
2 billion light-years

BRIGHTNESS: 4 trillion times brighter than the Sun

WEIGHT OF CENTRAL BLACK HOLE: 886 million Suns

LOCATION

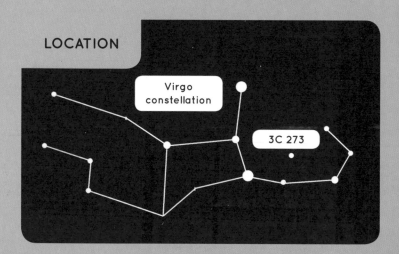

Virgo constellation

3C 273

3C 273 lies at the center of a giant elliptical (or egg-shaped) galaxy.

FIRST FIND

3C 273 was the first quasar to be identified, by astronomer Allan Sandage in the 1960s. It is the brightest quasar in our night sky and can sometimes be spotted in the Virgo constellation using a telescope. 3C 273 is so bright it is the most distant object you can see through a store-bought telescope.

In this *Hubble Space Telescope* photo, 3C 273 looks like a star, but it is really a distant galaxy.

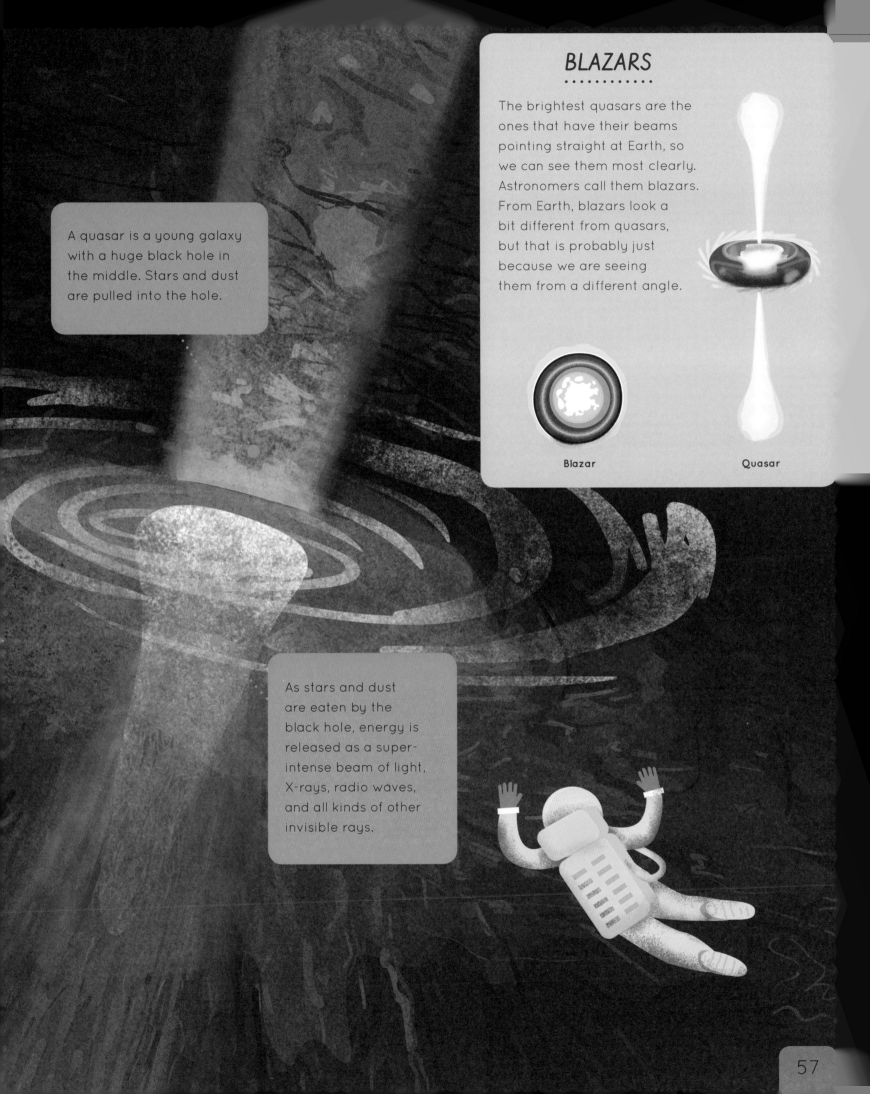

A quasar is a young galaxy with a huge black hole in the middle. Stars and dust are pulled into the hole.

BLAZARS

The brightest quasars are the ones that have their beams pointing straight at Earth, so we can see them most clearly. Astronomers call them blazars. From Earth, blazars look a bit different from quasars, but that is probably just because we are seeing them from a different angle.

Blazar

Quasar

As stars and dust are eaten by the black hole, energy is released as a super-intense beam of light, X-rays, radio waves, and all kinds of other invisible rays.

WEBB SPACE TELESCOPE

The most powerful telescopes we have on Earth and in space can see just over 13 billion light-years away. When it launches into space in 2019, the *James Webb Space Telescope* will change that—it will be able to see a massive 13.6 billion light-years away!

Remember that the farther away something is, the younger it looks to us, because its light and heat have taken so long to reach us. So astronomers can use the *Webb Telescope* to learn more about how stars and galaxies formed in the early days of the Universe. The telescope is a bit like a time machine!

SIZE: 69 ft wide

MIRROR: 21.3 ft wide

WEIGHT: 13,670 lb

DISTANCE FROM EARTH: 930,000 miles

COST: $10 billion

LAUNCH DATE: 2019

SCALE

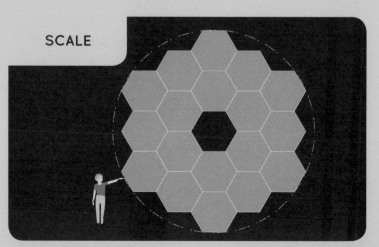

The telescope has a mirror made from 18 hexagons of beryllium metal coated in gold. The mirror catches the faint rays of heat coming from deep space and focuses them on a detector.

Present

If it gets warm, the *Webb Telescope* will not be able to pick up heat waves from far away stars. A shield the size of a tennis court blocks out heat from the Sun and even Earthshine, which is the light reflected from our planet.

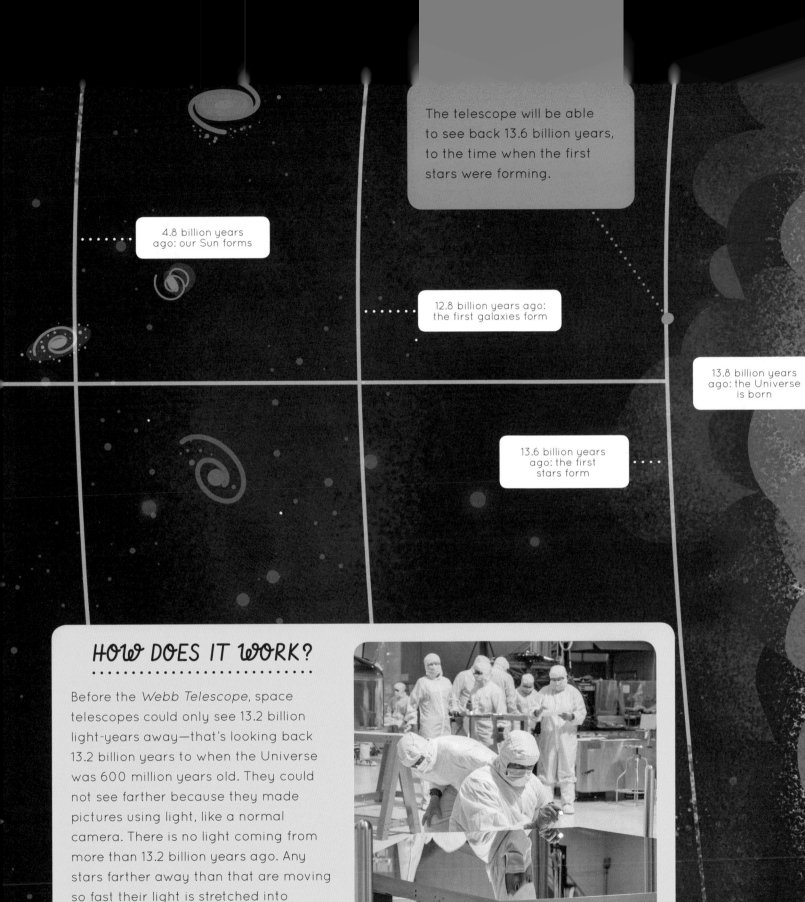

The telescope will be able to see back 13.6 billion years, to the time when the first stars were forming.

4.8 billion years ago: our Sun forms

12.8 billion years ago: the first galaxies form

13.8 billion years ago: the Universe is born

13.6 billion years ago: the first stars form

HOW DOES IT WORK?

Before the *Webb Telescope*, space telescopes could only see 13.2 billion light-years away—that's looking back 13.2 billion years to when the Universe was 600 million years old. They could not see farther because they made pictures using light, like a normal camera. There is no light coming from more than 13.2 billion years ago. Any stars farther away than that are moving so fast their light is stretched into **infrared** radiation (or heat). The *Webb Telescope* makes pictures out of this heat, like a night-time security camera.

A scientist examines one of the telescope's hexagonal mirrors for the slightest imperfection!

THE EDGE OF THE UNIVERSE

Is there an edge to the Universe? That's not an easy question to answer! The Universe began 13.8 billion years ago in a moment called the Big Bang. We have no idea what existed before that moment. In the Big Bang, the Universe started to expand from the tiniest pinprick— and has been getting bigger ever since.

We live in a bubble of space that is 13.8 billion light-years in all directions, but outside this is beyond the known Universe. Even though the Universe is growing in size, there is likely nothing outside it, not even the dimensions of length, breadth, and height, not even time!

The Universe is not always easy to understand, but the smartest people on Earth are trying to figure out the mysteries of space. Perhaps it will be you who solves them one day!

COSMIC MICROWAVES!

A **microwave** is a short kind of radio wave. A faint glow of microwaves fills the sky, called the Cosmic Microwave Background. It is all that is left of a flash of light that filled the Universe when it was just 380,000 years old. At that time, atoms of hydrogen gas formed throughout the Universe, creating a flash 100 times brighter than all the stars in the sky. Over the last 13.7 or so billion years, the light from that flash has stretched into invisible microwaves.

This picture of the Cosmic Microwave Background shows that the first atoms were not evenly spread through the Universe. Some places (shown in red and yellow) had more than others. These places became the walls of galaxy superclusters we see today.

You can listen to the echo of the Big Bang through a detuned radio. One crackle in 100 is made by leftover light from the Big Bang, stretched into radio waves over billions of years.

1 second: pure energy turns into particles such as electrons and protons.

3 minutes: the Universe is so hot and crowded with particles that there is no space left in between for light.

380,000 years: the first atoms form from electrons, protons, and neutrons, which releases a flash of light across the Universe.

200 million years: billions of stars begin to form.

Within the first seconds after the Big Bang, particles called **protons**, **electrons**, and neutrons had formed. Around 380,000 years later, the Universe had cooled down enough for these particles to join together to make the first atoms. Atoms are the tiny building blocks for everything in the Universe, from stars and planets to people.

1 billion years: the first planets form among the clouds of gas and dust spinning around stars.

GLOSSARY

acid Liquid chemical that burns other substances

asteroid Space rock

astronomical unit (AU) Distance from Earth to the Sun, around 93 million miles. Astronomers use the AU to measure the distances to other planets.

atmosphere Layer of gases that surrounds a planet or moon

atom Smallest unit of any substance

axis Imaginary line around which an object spins or rotates

billion A thousand million

black hole Very tiny but very heavy object in space. The gravity of a black hole is so strong that even beams of light cannot escape its pull.

constellation Pattern seen in the stars.

core Central region of a planet, star, or moon

dwarf planet Small globe that orbits the Sun but shares its orbit with other space rocks

electron Small particle found in atoms

equator Imaginary line that runs around the middle of a planet, star, or moon, sitting halfway between the north and south pole

event horizon Imaginary line around a black hole. Anything that crosses this line will be sucked inside.

galaxy Mass of stars that orbits around a central point. A galaxy contains at least several billion stars.

gamma ray Most powerful form of light-like radiation. We cannot see gamma rays but they contain so much energy they are very dangerous to us. Very bright galaxies and stars give out gamma rays but they

are blocked from damaging Earth by our atmosphere.

globule Cold, dark cloud of dust and gas. New stars are formed inside globules.

gravity Force that pulls all objects together. Earth's gravity pulls us down to the ground. The same force is holding the Moon in orbit around us, and holds galaxies together.

hemisphere Half of a globe, such as a planet

hypergiant Largest type of star, many hundreds of times wider than our Sun

infrared Name used for invisible heat waves. We cannot see them, but our skin does pick them up.

light-year Distance a beam of light travels in one year: 5,900 billion miles. We measure the distance between stars in light-years.

meteorite Space rock that has crashed into Earth. When this rock is flying through space, it is called a meteoroid. When it enters Earth's atmosphere, the rock begins to burn up, forming a meteor.

microwave Invisible radio wave with wavelengths measured in centimeters and millimeters. (Light wavelengths are much shorter. They are measured in nanometers, or billionths of a meter.)

Milky Way Our galaxy; the middle of the galaxy contains so many stars it forms a pale strip—or milky way—through the sky

moon Natural satellite that orbits a planet

nebula Fuzzy cloud of gas in deep space

neutron Small particle normally inside the core of an atom. The smallest stars in the Universe are made from pure neutrons.

orbit Path an object follows as it moves around larger objects. The Moon orbits Earth; Earth orbits the Sun; and the Sun orbits the center of the Milky Way (once every 230 million years).

particle Tiny object that groups together with other particles to make everything in the Universe

planet Large object that orbits a star. From Earth, planets look like stars but they move through the sky on a different path, showing us they are actually moving around the Sun.

pole Top or bottom point of a planet, star, or moon

proton Small particle inside the core of an atom. Protons have a positive electrical charge, while electrons have a negative one, which makes them attracted to each other. This attraction is what holds an atom together.

pulsar Small star that spins around very fast, giving out a flash of light or other radiation

quasar Very bright young galaxy near the edge of the Universe

radio wave Invisible light that has a very long wavelength

Solar System Local area of space around the Sun

star Super-hot ball of gas which produces light and heat

Sun Our Sun is the star around which the Earth orbits. It is the source of all our light and heat. A yellow dwarf star, it is about 863,700 miles across.

supermassive Enormously heavy. Supermassive objects weigh millions or even billions of times as much as the Sun.

telescope Device for seeing distant objects

trillion A million millions

X-ray Invisible high-energy ray given out by black holes and pulsars

INDEX